The Dominie Collection of Traditional Tales
For Young Readers

The Frog Prince

Retold by Alan Trussell-Cullen

Illustrated by David Preston Smith

Dominie Press, Inc.

Once upon a time, there was a very spoiled princess. She always did whatever she pleased. Her father, the king, gave her all kinds of toys and precious jewels.

Her favorite toy was a golden ball. The princess loved to throw it high into the air and catch it.

But then one day, the golden ball fell into a pond. The princess was very upset. She stamped her foot.

"I want my golden ball back," she said. "I will give all my precious jewels to anyone who can find it for me."

"I can help you," said a frog.

"You?! An ugly old frog?" said the princess.

"Of course," said the frog. "And I do not want your precious jewels."

"It's just as well," said the princess. "My precious jewels would not make you look any better!"

"Instead," said the frog, "I want you to grant me four wishes."
The princess frowned. "What are these wishes?" she asked.

"I want you to let me sit at your royal table, eat from your royal plate, drink from your royal cup, and sleep on your royal pillow for one whole night."

The princess was horrified. She wanted to say that she would never *ever* agree to the frog's wishes. But she wanted her golden ball back.

"I'll just pretend to agree," thought the spoiled princess.

As soon as the frog brought the ball to her, she turned and ran back to the castle as fast as she could.

The next day, there was a knock at the door. It was the frog!
"I have come to claim my wishes," said the frog.

The princess had to tell her father, the king, what had happened.
"If you made a promise," said the king, "then you must keep it!"

So that night, when the princess sat down to dinner, the frog sat right beside her.

He ate from her plate and drank from her cup.
"I feel sick!" said the princess. "I'm going to bed!"
"Not without me," said the frog. "You promised that I could sleep on your pillow."

The princess refused to look at the frog all night.

But in the morning, she opened one eye to take a peek. The frog was gone! And in its place, she saw a handsome, young prince.

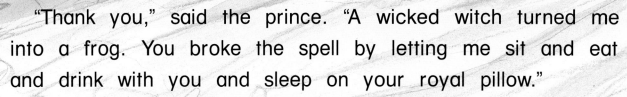

"Thank you," said the prince. "A wicked witch turned me into a frog. You broke the spell by letting me sit and eat and drink with you and sleep on your royal pillow."

The princess was amazed. It was the first time she had ever done something to help someone else. And she liked the feeling it gave her.

After that, the prince and the princess became good friends. They often played together.

In time they fell in love. They had a royal wedding and lived happily ever after.